Human Rights

SHELTER

Kate Haycock

Wayland

Titles in the Human Rights series
Clean Environment
Food
Freedom of Expression
Homeland
Justice
Shelter

Cover illustrations: *background* The New York skyline – the city has many homes and offices packed into a relatively small space; *inset* Homeless, cold and hungry in New York.

Editor: Deborah Elliott
Designer: Joyce Chester
Picture editor: Geraldine Nicholls

First published in 1993 by
Wayland (Publishers) Ltd
61 Western Road, Hove
East Sussex BN3 1JD
England

© Copyright 1993 Wayland (Publishers) Ltd

British Library Cataloguing in Publication Data
Haycock, Kate
Shelter. – (Human rights)
I. Title II. Series
363.5
ISBN 0 7502 0641 1

Typeset by Dorchester Typesetting Group Ltd
Printed and bound by Rotolito Lombarda S.p.A., Milan

Picture acknowledgements

Associated Press/Topham 16 (Dexter Creuz); Mary Evans Picture Library 9; Eye Ubiquitous cover inset, title page, 38; David Hoffman 23, 27, 31; Impact 4 (Peter Arkell), 5 (top), 12 (Sergio Dorantes), 13 (Piers Cavendish), 14 (Piers Cavendish/Reflex), 15 (Christophe Bluntzer), 17 (Mohamed Ansar), 22 (Paul Mattsson), 24 (Rachel Morton), 25 (top, Peter Arkell), 41 (John Arthur), 42 (Frank McGuigan), 44 (Peter Arkell), 45 (Billy Paddock); Popperfoto 7 (AFP), 18, 21, 23 (bottom, Vikter Korotayev), 26 (Philippe Wojazer), 29 (Pierre Boussel), 32 (Nancy McGirr), 34 (Manoocher), 36 (Jonathan Nourok), 43 (Kay Fisk); David Simson 6, 28; Tony Stone Worldwide 10 (Alena Vikova), 11 (Nicholas DeVore), 19 (Sue Cunningham), 37 (Julian Calder), 39 (Paul Chesley), 40 (James Strachan); Wayland Picture Library cover background, 5 (bottom, Jeff Greenberg), 30 (Jeff Greenberg).

Contents

1. A home to go to
page 4

2. A new problem?
page 7

3. The city as a magnet
page 10

4. Children on the streets
page 15

5. Ending up on the streets
page 22

6. No way out
page 28

7. The earthquake took my home
page 32

8. A sign of the times
page 37

9. What can be done?
page 42

Glossary
page 46

Further reading
page 47

Useful addresses
page 47

Index
page 48

1
A home to go to

In every country in the world, and for many different reasons, there are people living on the streets, sleeping out in the open. They are out in all weathers, when most of us are safe and warm at home. They are homeless.

Homelessness does not mean simply sleeping rough or living on the streets. Having a home is more than having a roof over your head and being protected from the elements (rain, snow etc). A home is something that belongs to you. You may not own it, but it is a place where you feel at home; a place where you are in control. It is yours; a place where you are entitled to be. A home is not just a place to sleep, it's a place to live.

Home is somewhere where we should be able to make plans, entertain friends, relax, spend time with our families and do our homework. For most of us it's the place we go back to after we've been shopping, working, attending school or college. Usually, our homes have kitchens where we can cook meals, bathrooms with running water, and electricity and heating.

The word 'home' can mean different things to different people. For this person, home is a couple of benches in a park in Hamburg, Germany. Tomorrow, home could be a different couple of benches, a shop doorway or a bus shelter.

This is what most of us think of as the perfect family scene: a family together, smiling, happy, warm and comfortable. The family is secure, protected by the walls that make up the home. Everyone has the right to a place where they can feel safe and secure.

Most of us could not imagine life without these 'basic essentials'. A home is something we take for granted. When we have a friend who is always out, we joke, 'Haven't you got a home to go to?' But for many people it's not a joke. They do not have homes. These people are not just somewhere else in the world, in poorer countries. They're not even just somewhere else in our own country: they may be only a few streets away. Why do we have homes when they do not?

The most visible signs of homelessness are the people who live and sleep on the streets of our cities, or in tents in our public parks. They have literally nowhere else to go. But there are also people who may have somewhere to sleep tonight, but who have no idea where they will sleep tomorrow night, or the night after that. Although they are homeless, they are much less visible than people sleeping on the streets because they disappear at night. Where do they go? Some find shelter in hostels run either by local authorities or by charities, which provide beds for a night and some hot food.

A homeless teenager looks out over the city of San Francisco in California, USA. There must be a home there for him, somewhere.

These people have bedded down for the night outside the SNCF train station in Paris, France. The ground makes a cold, hard mattress, and there is little protection from wind and rain.

The next morning they are turned out on to the streets again. Many people live by moving from hostel to hostel.

Some of the 'invisible' homeless stay with friends or relatives, sleeping on floors or sofas. Although this accommodation is safe and dry, it's temporary and it relies on the goodwill of others. Some people stay in 'bed and breakfast', boarding houses or houses shared with strangers, paid for by the government. Although these places provide much-needed roofs over people's heads, they are not ideal – they cannot be called home because the arrangements are only temporary.

Some homeless people disappear to temporary shelters or caravans. These makeshift dwellings are homes of sorts, but sometimes they leak, they fall down when it's windy, often they have no light, heat or running water, and usually they are small and cramped. They have been made into homes by people who have nowhere else to live. These people feel grateful to have somewhere to lie down at night, no matter how squalid or unpleasant the conditions. Would you want to live like that? Would anyone? Obviously the answer is no, so why should homeless people have to?

Some people choose to live 'on the road', travelling around and not settling in one place. But most people who live on the streets are there because of an unfortunate change in their circumstances, such as losing their jobs, not being able to keep up with their mortgage payments, or being thrown out by their parents. Instead of being looked after or helped, these people have to live on the streets with no comforts whatsoever.

2

A new problem?

HOMELESSNESS is not a new problem. In most countries in the past, governments did not provide any housing whatsoever. Individuals or communities were responsible for their own shelters, which, usually, they built themselves from natural materials such as wood, clay and straw. Often these shelters were brought down by winds or washed away by heavy rain, making the inhabitants homeless until they built new shelters.

Many of the causes of homelessness have been with us throughout history. People who work on the land are often dependent on landowners for places to live. In times of oppression they are often forced from their homes and driven off the land by the landowners. The Mayan Indians in Guatemala have had their land seized and have been forced to move to the remote hills to escape persecution. In the nineteenth century, Jews in parts of Eastern Europe were persecuted for their religious beliefs and were forced to leave their homes, and sometimes even their countries.

Civil wars have raged in Bosnia and Serbia since their separation from Yugoslavia. Serbian soldiers forced these Bosnian women to leave their homes. The women took only the belongings they could carry and set off to find refuge in another country.

7

War was, and still is, a major cause of homelessness. In some countries, a change in government or ruling party can result in members of the population having to leave their homes if, for example, they supported another political group. In 1992, former Yugoslavia was broken up into a number of separate states. Civil wars followed in many of the states, forcing people to leave their homes and villages and move to other areas. In the past, wars which lasted many years upset the entire pace of life and the economy of a country, causing the population to move about in search of work.

Bad harvests or economic depression are other major reasons why people leave their homes. In many countries in Africa, for example, terrible droughts frequently lead to famine, causing hundreds of thousands of people to walk long distances in search of food.

The Industrial Revolution, which took place in Europe in the eighteenth and nineteenth centuries, brought about the most significant change in the movement of people in the western world. Before the revolution, the majority of the population of Europe had been peasants, who worked on the land to produce food. New industrial inventions, the development of transport and the increase in world trade led to the growth of cities, built up around factories. These factories needed huge workforces; people were employed to work long hours and so needed to live close to their places of work. Houses were built specially for them near the factories.

Many people travelled to cities looking for work. Life on the land was hard and people heard that there were good jobs in the cities. But, after a while, there were not enough jobs for all the people who wanted, or needed, them. Without work people did not have money and could not pay for somewhere to live. This reduced many people to poverty, and having to scrape a living on the streets. Some received help from local churches and a few other charitable institutions, which struggled to cope with the growing numbers of poverty-stricken people.

In Britain, one of the first countries to undergo an industrial revolution, a law was introduced to deal with the problem. The Poor Law Amendment Act of 1834 ruled that no one would receive 'assistance from any quarter unless he (or she) entered the workhouse'. Workhouses were grim institutions where people who were starving and homeless received food and shelter in return for labour. The workhouses were not comfortable or welcoming places: the idea was that only utterly desperate people would end up there. It was seen as a disgrace

An illustration of a community workhouse in St Pancras, London, in the nineteenth century. It was women mostly who ended up in workhouses. In those days, few women had jobs and, without husbands or families, they had no means of support. Workhouses were dark and sombre places. 'Guests' had to work long hours in return for food and shelter. Still, it was better than being on the streets – just.

by society to end up in a workhouse, but many people found they had no other choice.

By the twentieth century, conditions were improving slowly as governments introduced laws protecting workers and more affordable homes were built. The problem of homelessness did not disappear, however.

In 1933, the famous English author, George Orwell, wrote a book called *Down and Out in Paris and London*, in which he described the lives of the down-and-outs in the two cities. To research his book, Orwell lived as a tramp for a short time. He discovered the appalling way in which tramps were treated. Tramps could spend only one night in any given period in a hostel or doss-house. So they 'tramped' across the country to hostels in nearby towns, and so on, constantly on the move.

Most of Orwell's fellow tramps were single men, who had lost their roots, had turned to drink, or actually preferred the wandering lifestyle to a more settled routine. People regarded them as either lazy or misfits and, although there were a fair number of tramps, their situation was not regarded as a huge problem. Most people preferred to forget about the existence of tramps.

3

The city as a magnet

As in Western Europe 150 years ago, the phenomenon of people moving to cities in search of work can be seen today in developing countries in Latin America, Asia and Africa. Peasant farmers are leaving their homes in the country and going to cities where, many believe, they will find their fortunes. For some people the move is a desperate measure: they hope that they will find work to support themselves and their hungry families.

Meanwhile cities grow larger and larger. Today the problem is made worse by the population explosion; the number of people in the world is growing at a frightening rate. Thanks to advances in medicine and more awareness of hygiene and sanitation, people are living longer. More and more people are competing for the same amount of land.

When cities grow too quickly there is an urgent need for more housing for the huge influx of new workers. The authorities in most cities do not have the funds to create lots of housing overnight. The growth in industry means that more factories and offices are built. The demand for land means the price goes up; land which may have been used to build housing for

Most of the cities in the world are growing. New shops and office blocks are being built on land which could have been used for housing. In fact, many houses in cities are being knocked down to make way for new office blocks.

These children are working at a dye factory in Morocco. They work long hours and are paid very little.

workers may now be more valuable for building offices. In the fight for space, the working classes are usually forgotten. They cannot afford to pay the high rents in the cities so they move to the outskirts. There the land is cheaper but the journey to and from work is much longer. Soon, accommodation in the outskirts becomes scarce and new arrivals find it harder and harder to find places to live which they can afford. Some stay with friends until they find places of their own. Others may have to live on the streets until they find somewhere to live.

As more people move to cities, there is less work to go round. Few jobs provide real security. Employers exploit the labour force because there are more workers than jobs. Workers are expected to put up with poor working conditions and long hours for little money. They do not get paid if they are sick, and if they have to take a day off they may find that someone else has stepped into their shoes.

When a factory closes down several hundred people are suddenly out of work in the same area, all desperately needing new jobs. Their families will starve if they do not find something soon – anything. Many find themselves accepting work which pays almost nothing. But these people find they have no choice other than to be used as cheap labour. If they do not take the jobs, there are others, even more desperate, who will and the employers know that. For people who cannot find even cheap labour there is often no other choice but to give up their homes. If they are new to the city, they have no roots there, or families to help them out. It is very easy for their lives to fall apart.

Mexico City, the capital of Mexico, is one of the largest cities in the world, with over 20 million inhabitants. It has grown at an alarming rate and is a busy, dirty, noisy, crowded place. It takes a lot of time and money to build schools, hospitals and other facilities for the growing population. There is not enough time to build new roads to cope with the strain of increasing traffic. And, most importantly, there are too few houses for the number of people living in Mexico City.

One of the reasons for the rapid increase in population in Mexico City was the growth of new industry which needed workers in the factories. Poor people from the surrounding countryside were attracted to the city by promises of good wages and a better standard of living. In the early days people fared well. They earned plenty of money, enough even to send some back home to their families in the countryside. They returned home with stories of the great city, which encouraged others to follow.

Assembling a stove at a factory in Mexico City. Mexico City is an example of a city in which industry has expanded rapidly. However, while the number of factories in Mexico City has grown, the number of houses in the city has fallen.

Ramón and Maria were tempted by the stories of Mexico City and the good life they believed it had to offer them and their two children. Ramón and Maria loved their village and the close-knit family which they had known all their lives. They did not want to leave and go to a city where they did not know anyone. But jobs in the village were scarce and farmers were being paid less and less for their produce. Eventually the couple decided to take the plunge and go to Mexico City for a couple of years. There, they would try to save enough money to enable them to return to the village and buy some land on which to build a house.

In the beginning everything went well for Ramón and Maria. Ramón found work in a factory and Maria worked in a laundry. They had enough money to rent a small flat with a separate bedroom for the children. In fact, things seemed to be working out so well for the family that, after two years, they decided not to return to the village; the children would get a better education in the city. Ramón saved enough money from working overtime to buy a small plot of land on which to build a house. He bought an old van and did some extra work in the evening delivering to factories.

A shanty town in Mexico City.

Everything seemed perfect until one evening when Ramón did not return home. Maria found out that he had had an accident in his van and had been taken to hospital. It was terrible news; Ramón was paralysed from the waist downwards. He could not walk, he could not drive, he could not work.

The family did not receive any money from either the factory owners or the state. Before long they had to sell everything in order to buy food. Eventually they had to sell their home and move into a rented apartment. Within a few weeks the family did not have enough money to pay the rent.

As far as the city planners in Mexico City are concerned, the shanty towns, which appear almost overnight, do not exist.

Although Maria worked hard at the laundry and Ramón tried to do repair work at home, they could not make ends meet. The landlord was sympathetic but he had a family too; he evicted Ramón, Maria and the children.

Now the family was homeless. They spent the first night at the bus station. They had just enough money for the journey back to their village. A few years before, the family had left the village feeling optimistic, excited and proud. They returned home ashamed and downtrodden. Maria's mother put them up in her house and, very slowly, they struggled to rebuild their life in the country.

Ramón and Maria were lucky. At least they had families to turn to. Many people do not. They either have no families or are too proud to return home, begging for help. Perhaps their families do not have the means to help.

There are many people with stories like Ramón and Maria's. Each story is different: factories close down so people lose their jobs; the breadwinner of a family is injured or even dies; a family falls into debt. It is easy to become homeless, because when you have a very low income, or none at all, even the most basic type of housing is too expensive. Low-paid jobs, such as polishing shoes, taking in washing or selling lottery tickets, might bring in enough money to buy food, but not to pay rent.

4
Children on the streets

In many parts of the world there are children who have no homes and no families. These children have to fend for themselves as best they can.

Ravi is one such child. He is eleven years old and has never been to school, although he would love to learn to read and write. He has no family. He and his older sister, Yasmin, were abandoned by their parents when Ravi was a young baby. Since then, Ravi's 'home' has been the streets of Bombay, a large city in India.

Ravi sees Yasmin every now and then; the man she lives with does not want Ravi to live with them. Ravi does not like the man anyway and does not want to live in his house. He is used to life on the streets. His friends are there and, although he wears ragged clothes and has no shoes, Ravi is reasonably healthy. But don't get the wrong idea: Ravi's life is harsh and brutal, and without any comforts.

He and Yasmin used to sit outside shops and beg for money to buy food.

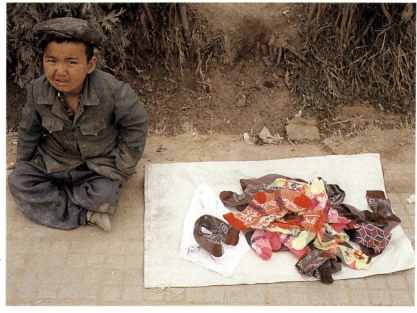

Life on the streets is hard, especially for children. This boy lives on the streets of Kashgar in China. He sells goods at the side of the road to earn money to buy food.

Occasionally they ran errands for shopkeepers to earn some extra money. While living on the streets, Ravi has learned how to make a living. Sometimes he asks people for money outright, or he offers to show tourists some sights in return for a tip: a lot of people tell him to go away, of course. He is popular with most of the local shopkeepers and business owners, and is often given odd jobs to do – cleaning, running errands or washing up.

Ravi is always looking for ways to earn money, such as selling tea or bags for local traders.

Ravi and some of his friends sell tea. This is very common in India where, because it is so hot, people drink lots of tea. Rather than go into a restaurant or tea-shop, they buy it on the street from the young boys who run around with tea-trays. Ravi is based at a shop, where the tea is made and the cups are washed after use. He is the 'salesman', so he provides the shopkeeper with a good service in return for a small share of the profits. His share never amounts to very much.

Although there is free schooling in India, Ravi could never consider going since he has to spend his days looking for ways to earn money or find food. This is a full-time job. There is no shortage of children like Ravi to provide very cheap labour for all the shops and businesses of Bombay. He only earns enough money to feed himself, although he tries to save up. Ravi's greatest dream is that one day he will be able to buy his own rickshaw so that he can earn a good living.

Ravi's bed is in an alleyway. He has an old blanket which he lies on when the weather is hot. Sometimes he finds some old newspaper or packaging, which is more comfortable. Anyway, after a long hard day, Ravi does not have a problem sleeping. Ravi shares the alleyway with a few other children. They chat and joke about their day, but before long they fall asleep.

This cobbler and his family left the countryside in the hope of a better life in Bombay.

It is hard for Ravi to have any possessions: he has nowhere to put them. If he leaves anything in the alleyway, someone will come along and take it. Even his friends steal from one another. Ravi once asked his sister to look after a few rupees he had saved up. One day when he went to visit her, Yasmin told him that the man she was living with had found the money and had taken it from her. Now Ravi keeps his money with him, or hides it in a secret place.

This way of life is typical in Indian cities. Most of the 900 million people in India are peasants who live in villages in the countryside and work on the land. This is a very poor way of life, but people survive because they have large families who help each other. Sometimes, however, if the crops fail, people leave their homes and go to the city to seek work. Some members of large families are sent away to earn their own keep, as there is not enough land to support everyone. Sometimes a son or daughter falls out with his or her parents and decides to run away.

Children keeping warm by a fire in New Delhi, the capital city of India. Tens of thousands of homeless children live on the streets of this city alone. The government of India tries to pretend the children don't exist.

All these people go to cities looking for work. Unless they are lucky, or they know someone with whom they can stay, they will probably end up in one of the shanty towns or slums which are found in all of India's cities. The shanty towns are on pieces of wasteland, often on the outskirts of the cities. People build shacks from bits of material, such as tin, cardboard or wood, which they find on rubbish tips. The shanty towns are overcrowded and, because there is no running water or toilets, disease and infection spread easily. These conditions may sound intolerable to us, but for the people who live there, there is usually no other choice: the shanty towns are their homes. As in the countryside, people keep chickens and goats outside their huts and live as near to normal lives as possible.

Slums are old buildings which are in poor condition. They provide cheap accommodation but are often overcrowded and unhealthy. Slums and shanty towns are an embarrassment to the government, but demolishing them, as the former Prime Minister of India, Indira Gandhi, did in Delhi, leaves the greater problem and expense of rehousing all the people who lived there. It is easier to leave them alone, as long as they are out of the way of tourists and the richer inhabitants of the city who would complain about the way the buildings looked. About one-third of city dwellers cannot find or afford proper accommodation. Many people with jobs have to sleep on the streets. Taxi drivers often sleep in their cars. In some cities even the slums are short of space and landlords rent out *bustees*, which are basic tents.

India is a poor country with a huge population. The government faces a never-ending task of trying to provide for everyone. For people like Ravi, life is a day-to-day struggle for survival. In many ways Ravi is one of the luckier street children. Although he has no possessions and no education, he has learned to adapt to life on the streets. He is bright, healthy, likeable and works hard. But what would happen to him if he became sick? Who would care for him? What does his future hold? What if he wants to get married and have a family? Will he bring his children up on the streets? Will he grow old on the streets? Will he die there? Ravi does not have time to worry about these questions.

For many children, left to look after themselves on the streets of a city, the strains are hard to cope with. The society in which they fight for survival is cut-throat. There is no trust, possessions have to be hidden or guarded fiercely and, it seems, there is no way out. It is hardly surprising that many children become involved in crime or prostitution. Girls and boys alike are

The photograph is of Rio de Janeiro in Brazil. In the foreground is one of the city's many shanty towns, where homeless people live in makeshift shelters without water or sewage facilities. In the distance is the city's centre of wealth and industry.

exploited by people who persuade them to sell their bodies for sex, or to sell drugs. Children are forced into activities which lead to either physical harm or trouble with the police.

A similar problem exists on the other side of the world. It is estimated that 8 million children live on the streets of Brazil's cities. Many have been abandoned at birth by uneducated parents, who did not know about birth control and who could not afford to feed a new baby. Many are from families who live on the streets – these children know no other life.

Brazil's is one of the most unequal societies in the world. The rich live in fabulous houses on beaches, such as the famous Copacabana, with lavish lifestyles. In contrast, only a few streets away from the homes of these 'beautiful people', children beg, peddle goods such as penny sweets and peanuts, or collect rubbish in order to get enough to eat. They eat rotting food which has been thrown out by shops or restaurants. Many turn to crime at a very young age and, as in India, are open to exploitation. Brazil has no state welfare system and the underclass of poor people is so huge that any attempts to improve their situation makes only a very small impression.

Brazil has a much more violent society than India. The children are forced to work for gangs, criminals and even corrupt police officers, and their lives are in danger if they refuse. They quickly learn the art of survival, like the gang of child pickpockets used by Fagin, in *Oliver Twist*.

As if this wasn't enough, the children now face another danger. The citizens of the streets which the children call home have had enough. Shopkeepers, business owners and residents want them cleared away because they feel the children are harmful to trade and tourism. So some have resorted to killing the children who litter their doorways and pavements, who cause a nuisance begging and who, without even knowing it, introduce violent crime to the areas.

It is estimated that at least one child a day is killed on the streets of Rio de Janeiro in Brazil. During the night, cars prowl the streets and mow down victims at random with machine guns. Often the police are corrupt and are paid not to investigate the murders. Witnesses are paid to keep quiet, or threatened if they try to speak out. Many citizens either do not know about the killings or prefer to pretend they don't know. Others do not see the children as human beings but as lice or vermin which should be destroyed. They do not care about children who are caught in a situation from which they cannot escape. Now the children live in fear for their lives.

Many countries have special organizations set up to protect children and keep them off the streets. Families and single mothers are given priority for housing. But Brazil and India are just two of many examples of countries which do not provide for their children. There, many children are born into unequal societies with no homes, no security, often no families (they are abandoned at birth), and no opportunities for education. Knowing no better, they simply look for ways to get food and to survive.

Three eight-year-old boys sit handcuffed to a sink in the Fortaleza bus station in northern Brazil. The police caught the boys begging.

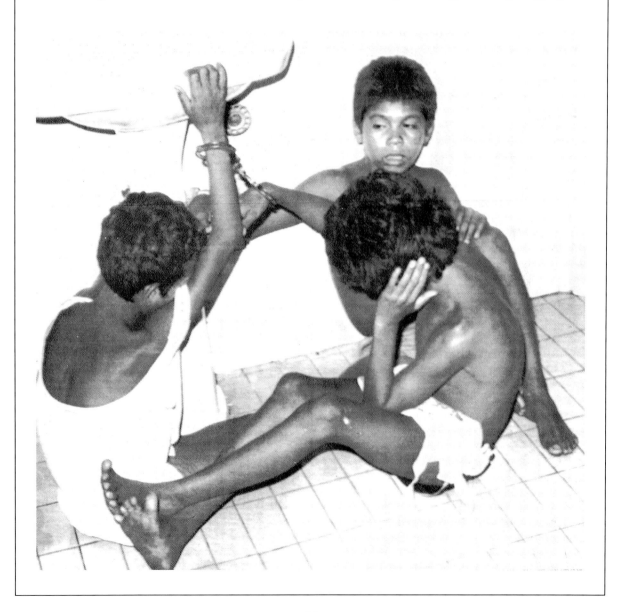

5

Ending up on the streets

HOMELESSNESS is not just a problem in developing countries or something which happened years ago, in the days that George Orwell wrote about. Most people in developed countries are much better off now than at any other time in the past. Many even have the luxury of social services; these are government departments specially set up to look after people's needs. However, despite all this, the amount of homeless people in developed countries is growing. Who are the homeless people of these so-called developed countries?

Alistair is from Scotland. He has never known his parents. Up until the age of sixteen, Alistair lived in a number of different children's homes. He hated the rules in the homes and was determined to leave as soon as he could. Some of his friends from the children's home had already left and gone to live in London. They wrote to Alistair and told him he could stay with them and they would help him try to find work.

Alistair was excited at the prospect of going to London and, when he

A child sits at the window of a squat – an empty building which is used as a home. The people living in this squat are about to be evicted by the council.

turned sixteen, he set off to find his friends. What they had not told him was that they lived in a squat – an empty house which they had broken into illegally and made into a home.

This picture captures the misery of losing your home. The family has been evicted from a squat. Now the family faces life on the streets: no security, no warmth, no shelter.

But there was plenty of space and Alistair was made welcome.

He managed to find a job working in a pizza parlour. Although he had to work late at night, the people there were really friendly and at least he had money to spend on going out to the cinema and discos occasionally. Alistair also liked the people that he met through his friends in the squat.

After a few months, though, the people in the squat started getting letters from the local council, saying that they were going to be evicted as they should not be living there. Dan, one of the people who had lived in the squat for a long time, was not worried. He said that they had been threatened before, but nothing had ever come of it. One night, however, Alistair came home from work to find the place completely boarded up and no one inside. People from the council had come to the squat and evicted everyone living there.

Dan had a friend who lived in another squat, so the next day he and Alistair asked if they could sleep on the floor. For the next few months, Alistair slept on friends' floors, a few days here, a few weeks there. Often he had to sleep in the living room, so he couldn't go to bed until everyone else did, and he was woken up as soon as someone got up. He went to work tired and came back tired. When he had the energy he tried to find somewhere more permanent to live.

He went along to the local council and asked if there were any council flats available. He was told there was a waiting list of five years, and that priority was always given to people with children, the elderly or the disabled.

Alistair tried to rent a room in a flat, but was told he had to pay a large deposit and one month's rent in advance, and he could not save that much money from his wages.

Although the manager of the pizza parlour liked him, the business was not doing very well, so Alistair only worked when he was needed. Sometimes he only worked one or two shifts a week. One day, when he was finishing his shift, the manager told him that he was very sorry but he didn't need Alistair to work there anymore. There simply was not enough money to pay his wages. Alistair was desperate but he still had a bit of money to live on. Now he was looking for a job and somewhere to live. He went to the social security office, where an officer advised him to go back to his parents: parents Alistair had never known.

Now Alistair lives on the streets. He begs for enough money to eat, and he sleeps in doorways. Alistair is neither lazy nor a criminal. He does not deserve to be homeless – no one does. He is simply one of the victims of a society which does not always provide for its more unfortunate members.

There are many young people in Alistair's situation today. Many leave children's homes as soon as they can legally (the age of sixteen). Some even run away before this. They have had no experience of secure family life and

Alistair left Scotland for a new and, what he hoped would be, better life in London. Now he lives on the streets, begging for money from passers-by. His dreams, like those of so many like him, have been shattered.

are not prepared for the big wide world. Other young people have unhappy homes – they may argue with their parents or they may come from homes where, as soon as they are old enough to work, they are kicked out and made to fend for themselves. They naïvely go to big cities where they think they will find jobs and places to live. When they get there, usually their dreams, like Alistair's, are shattered.

Left *Today there are two cities in London. One is the London of Buckingham Palace, restaurants and houses. The other is what is known as 'Cardboard City', made up of the makeshift shelters of the homeless.*

Below *An elderly homeless man spends his days drinking vodka in a Moscow train station.*

These people are vulnerable, they have nowhere to go. They are open to all sorts of trouble: they get mixed up with a bad set; they may be persuaded to turn to crime, or to dabble with drugs. Girls innocently accept offers of work in return for a place to live and find themselves working as prostitutes. Boys too are tempted into prostitution. No one does this unless they are desperate. It is a sleazy, shady, mean way of life, where young, helpless people are exploited by unsavoury characters and are often unable to escape.

While the plight of young people is particularly tragic, there are many other groups of people who live on the city streets. Some are married women whose violent husbands made their lives so miserable that the women had to get away. These women have to leave their own homes because of brutal men; anything is better than putting up with beatings and arguments. They leave but they have nowhere to go.

There are alcoholics and drug addicts living on the streets, too. There are many reasons why people end up as alcoholics and drug addicts.

Some people think it's because they simply like drink or drugs. Sadly, the reasons are usually much more tragic. Most alcoholics and drug addicts have ended up in their particular situation because they felt they had failed in life or because they were miserable or depressed. Once addicted to drink or drugs, it becomes almost impossible to hold down a job or lead a normal life. Some spend time in rehabilitation clinics where their addiction is treated, but when they come out they may have nowhere to go but the streets. They try to make their existence more bearable by drinking or taking drugs again. After a while, the clinics refuse to take them, as they are 'beyond help', or they themselves believe they are lost causes and stop seeking help.

Some people from other countries have problems living in developed countries. Some left their homes because of wars or oppressive governments in their own countries. They thought that they could start a new life by moving to another country. But, having arrived in the new country, many find they are not accepted by the majority of the population. They are treated as outsiders or as inferior. They have trouble speaking the language so it is difficult for them to find employment. Without jobs and without prospects of finding jobs, many lose faith in themselves. There is no one to turn to.

Some of the people living on the streets are former inmates of prisons. Many leave prison hoping for a fresh start, and intending to lead a life without crime, to work hard and do well. But their criminal records make most employers wary about giving the former prisoners work and, often, their friends and families do not want to associate with them anymore. They feel worthless.

A woman hangs out clothes to dry at a squatters' camp in Paris. The people living in the camp are migrants from North Africa, who came to Paris seeking shelter.

There are a number of mentally ill people living on the streets of developed countries. The authorities in these countries have decided that it is better for mentally ill people of a certain age to live in the community rather than in special homes where they are looked after by trained staff. So many people with psychological problems find themselves turned out of mental institutions and having to fend for themselves. Some manage very well. Others have no idea how to care for themselves, as people have always looked after them. Many end up on the streets, roaming aimlessly.

This woman is mentally ill and in need of medical help. Instead she lives on the streets of Edinburgh, Scotland.

One by one these people swell the numbers of the homeless. But each one is an individual with different problems and distinct needs. They all need advice and help which they do not always receive. The streets of our big cities are becoming human dustbins, where the people go who are forgotten by society. Most of them are on the streets because, when they had problems or made mistakes, there was no one there to help them.

6

No way out

MOST people who have ended up living on the streets, without shelter, find that the way out can be very difficult, if not impossible.

Claudette lives on the streets of Paris. She says, 'Living on the streets affects how you look. There is nowhere to wash yourself or your hair or your clothes, so you get really dirty and smelly. Most of us [people on the streets] don't have many clothes anyway – I sold all mine except what I'm wearing. So I couldn't really clean these clothes even if I had the money to go to the launderette.

'You get dirtier than normal anyway, sitting and lying on the pavements, and from the pollution from the traffic. I can't afford a haircut, so my hair looks untidy even if I do wash it, which isn't very often. Most of the guys who live on the streets grow long beards, which some people think makes them look frightening.

'I eat what I can find. People sometimes give me food, or I find food in rubbish bins or outside restaurants. There are places where you can get hot meals sometimes – charities and soup kitchens. When I get some money to buy food, obviously I get the cheapest thing that's going to fill me up – bread or chips. It's hardly a healthy diet of fresh fruit and vegetables!

His sign tells passers-by that he is hungry and alone and needs help. He wants a job and a home, too. Who could or should help him?

A homeless woman and her son sleep on a Parisian street. It is winter, a particularly cold winter which has caused the deaths of eight people who lived on the streets. They had no protection from the cold. This woman and child have only a few blankets.

'Because we are out in all weathers, cold and wet, many of us get ill a lot. Most of my friends already have quite bad arthritis from the cold. Sleep is a problem. Like everyone else here, I sleep when I can: often I get woken up by the cold or the rain. I try to block out the light by pulling my blanket over my head. It's noisy too with all the traffic.

'What I don't understand is why people [not homeless] push or kick us. The police try to get us to move along sometimes. Though, to be honest, most of the time they leave us alone. Every now and then a dog pees on me while I'm asleep. There are rats as well, and insects, but they don't bother me much anymore. You can get used to most things in the end. Yes, it's hard to get a good night's sleep.

'All in all it's pretty difficult to look good when you live on the streets. People try to avoid you: they just see the dirt, not the person underneath. I have tried to find work – in a restaurant or a kitchen usually, not an office. But the bosses don't even want to talk to me because I look such a sight and I probably smell. They certainly wouldn't want to spend the day working with me.

'Anyway, because we look like this, people think that the homeless are not capable of doing anything very well. They blame us for how we look. They don't realize that our situation makes it impossible for us to keep clean and tidy. After a little while it's not just our appearance or our health that suffer. The way people treat us begins to have an effect. You forget that really it's just because you're not able to wash, and start thinking it's your fault. Maybe we are inferior to everyone else! You lose confidence. What little you have left, that is, after losing a job, or whatever brought you to this situation. You begin to feel that you are not capable of having a job. You are very conscious of how you look and are frightened of approaching people.

'I carry everything I own around with me. You can't leave anything you don't want to lose or it will be stolen. So you just keep what you can carry. Anyway, carrying lots of stuff around can be a problem. Some people use supermarket trolleys, but I like to be able to get about quickly.

Most homeless people have to carry their belongings around as they search for tonight's shelter. If they leave anything lying around, it could be stolen.

'I'm used to living on the streets. Sometimes I stay in one of the hostels. But you don't get much sleep sharing a room with ten or more others. I used to go to hostels more than I do now, because I felt safer staying in them. Some of the men living on the streets get violent, but I've learned how to handle them. They're worst when they've been drinking. I have the odd drink, but I'm not dependent, thank goodness. The people who are have a terrible time. It's a way of living in your own world though.

'I had a bad case of bronchitis this winter. There are some really kind doctors who work at free clinics where people like me are treated. They [the doctors] gave me some medicine; they treated me like I was a human being.'

There are some free clinics in Paris where homeless people can be treated by doctors.

Claudette would like to stop living on the streets. For a while she looked for work, but had no success, probably because of the way she looked. No one gave her a chance. Now, she has given up. It is easy for people to say, 'Why don't the homeless help themselves? Why don't they do something about their situation?' Unfortunately, for homeless people, helping themselves is a lot harder than it would be for people with homes, cars, jobs, and telephones, not to mention bathrooms, clean clothes and healthy food. The way of life for the homeless is so difficult it weakens them, and many lose their spirit. Who can they turn to for help? Who will listen?

When people lose their homes, they lose their dignity, their vote, their rights. They have no power and no economic strength. They no longer seem to count in society. While there may be a few people who choose to lead wandering lives, the majority of homeless people would prefer not to be homeless, but to have shelter. Most people become homeless through no fault of their own, when a stroke of bad luck befalls them, crushing their attempts to live honest, hard-working lives. For many homeless people there is simply no way out.

7

The earthquake took my home

HURRICANES, floods, tidal waves, landslides, avalanches, volcanoes and earthquakes are natural disasters which can devastate whole communities. As well as killing people, they also leave homes destroyed or badly damaged and in need of repair. It takes time to repair or rebuild homes. Meanwhile, the occupants are homeless.

On 10 October, 1986, an enormous earthquake shook the centre of El Salvador in Central America. The capital city, San Salvador, was hit particularly badly. Ana and her family lived in one of the city's slums where the houses were flimsy, with heavy tiled roofs.

Trying to get on with life after the earthquake in El Salvador.

What now? Roseina de Los Angeles holds her daughter, Marcella. It is eight days after the earthquake destroyed her home in San Salvador.

When the earthquake hit, Ana was playing with her brothers outside in the street. She felt the rumble of the tremor and was very frightened. She wanted to run inside the house, but luckily her brother pulled her away. A few seconds later, there was a great crash and her house fell down. She screamed because her mother and grandmother were inside. The walls had been shaken so badly they had collapsed, bringing the heavy roof down on top of the two women inside. Where Ana's little house had stood, there was now a big pile of rubble. All around them other houses were also collapsing.

Ana was one of more than 150,000 people made homeless by the earthquake. Her mother and grandmother were among more than 1,000 people who were killed. A further 10,000 people were injured. Ana and her brothers were helped by money from a fund, which was made up of donations sent by richer nations to give instant relief to those in need. Medical care, food and bedding were provided and temporary shelters were erected. But the more long-term task of rebuilding the city was forgotten by the rest of the world, once the immediate needs were seen to.

The earthquake hit when El Salvador was in the middle of a devastating civil war. This war had brought about 60,000 deaths in seven years, and had caused one million people to leave El Salvador and take refuge from the violence in neighbouring countries.

The war also meant that a lot of money had been spent on fighting instead of growing food and producing goods to sell abroad. The government did not have the money necessary to rebuild all the destroyed houses.

The makeshift shelters which people made from rubble, corrugated iron and wood for temporary use are now their homes. Many of the shanty towns have no running water, no electricity, poorer sewage and dirt roads. There is also a problem of overcrowding.

Demonstrations in Cairo after the earthquake in 1992.

Today, Ana and her brothers and father are still living in a makeshift shack in one of these shanty towns. They hope that one day the government of El Salvador will find the money to build them a new home.

The earthquake that shook Cairo, the capital of Egypt, in the summer of 1992, was similarly devastating. It affected the poorer parts of the city, where people lived in slums. These had been built very badly and had been kept in a poor state of repair, because the landlords who owned the houses could not afford to maintain them. When the earthquake hit, these

slum dwellings collapsed like a house of cards. Meanwhile in outlying villages, where the impact of the earthquake was also severe, 25,000 people were made homeless when their two-storey mud and brick houses were demolished instantly. Many of these people ended up sleeping rough.

Millions of dollars of international aid was sent to help the victims of the Cairo earthquake. However, most of the money went to people in the city, while those outside received only a few tents, and money was only available to the families of those killed or injured. Many people had to live in the open and were given no money or help. This led to demonstrations in the streets and battles between the police and people angry about the slow response of the authorities to the problem of homelessness. People blamed the government.

It is not only in poor countries where natural disasters cause homelessness. Naples, in southern Italy, is in the middle of an area prone to earthquakes and volcanic eruptions. In November 1980, an earthquake caused the deaths of 2,570 people in the region and left 120,000 people homeless. Most of these were from poor neighbourhoods in the old town. Six years later, some 4,500 families were still living in public buildings such as schools, or in hotels.

San Francisco in California is situated very close to a huge fault in the earth which makes earthquakes a regular occurrence. The city has experienced some devastating earthquakes. For example, in 1906 San Francisco was almost destroyed by an earthquake and the resulting fire, which exposed the weaknesses of many of the buildings. The authorities in the city have gradually introduced stricter building regulations, to make the city 'earthquake-proof'. However, in November 1989 an earthquake brought down 23,000 houses.

Smoke billows from a section of a motorway in San Francisco, which collapsed after the earthquake hit the city in 1989. Homes, office blocks and motorways were all destroyed.

People who lost their homes and belongings in the San Francisco earthquake pick through donated clothing.

On this occasion, many of the buildings that were destroyed were old and in fairly poor parts of the city. The homeless population of San Francisco was affected particularly badly because many of their hostels had to close, halving the number of available beds. These are people who have no alternatives. Some people could stay with friends or family or, if they had enough money, stay in a hotel. Poor people had to make do with the street or temporary shelters, such as tents. In one town near San Francisco which was badly hit by the earthquake, 100 families spent the winter living in tents. Eventually they were rehoused.

Poor quality housing collapses easily, so it is more likely to be destroyed in the event of a natural disaster. Good quality housing is not only less likely to fall down, thus saving money in the long run, but it also provides better living conditions. The problem is that strong, well-built, earthquake-proof houses cost a lot of money to build. Unfortunately, as we have seen, the money is often not available, governments are able only to provide temporary solutions.

8
A sign of the times

A shortage of housing is one of the reasons why people are homeless. Surely if governments built more homes, there would be no more homelessness? Unfortunately, as society changes, the number of homes needed also changes. This is because as a society becomes wealthier, the more people's expectations increase. The more wealth people have, the more likely they are to want larger houses. In some countries it is not unusual for one person to live alone in a house with several bedrooms! Divorced couples double the demand for housing when they move out of their shared house into two individual houses.

In the past, young people used to live in their parents' home for a long time. Today it is accepted, and even expected, that they will move out and be independent. Many are made to leave home by their parents, who are fed up looking after them.

An aerial view of a suburb of Manchester in northern England.

Budapest in Hungary is one of the many cities in the world with a problem of overcrowding. No new houses are being built, and accommodation becomes available only when the occupant dies.

Laszlow lives in Budapest, the capital of Hungary. Like many young people all over the world, he wants a place of his own. However, there is a severe housing shortage in Budapest. Houses only become available when someone dies. Young people are at the bottom of the list of priorities.

A few years ago, Laszlow took advantage of a scheme which enabled him to move out of his parent's home and jump to the top of the list. As there are many old people living alone who are in need of company or some basic care, the Hungarian government came up with the idea of matching them up with young people. Laszlow moved into the home of an old man who, although healthy, was quite frail. He was a companion to the old man, and also helped him by running errands, doing the shopping, cooking and cleaning.

Laszlow and the old man got on very well. Laszlow didn't mind helping him out, because it meant he was free to lead his own life. They lived together for three years, until the man became sick and went to hospital. After a few weeks, he died. Laszlow was very upset, but the scheme now allowed him to take over the tenancy of the house. Because he had helped out the authorities by relieving the burden of its care for the elderly, Laszlow was now rewarded with his own home.

However, the scheme was not a total success. Many of the young people who took part in the scheme got more than they had bargained for. One of Laszlow's friends, Sophie, had to bathe and feed the old woman she moved in with. This old woman, although totally dependent on Sophie for help, was strong and would live for many more years. Understandably many of the old people resented the young people being in their homes, and felt they were waiting for them to die!

Some newly married couples continue to live with one or other's parents after getting married. This is particularly true in some cultures. In others, many young couples want to set up their own homes as soon as possible.

Chunying and Lanying live in Shanghai, China's most densely populated city with 13 million inhabitants.

A view of a crowded apartment building in Shanghai, China.

Chunying and Lanying have been married for two years and are currently living in Chunying's parents' house, with Chunying's three brothers and sisters. His grandmother lives in the house too.

It is really crowded in Chunying's house and he and Lanying never have much privacy. They have been on a waiting list for a flat of their own ever since they decided to get married. The problem is, they are not the only couple on the list. There are hundreds of thousands of Shanghainese on the official waiting list, but the real number is probably much higher.

In Communist China, most people have jobs. Affording somewhere to live is not a problem as housing is subsidized (the government puts money towards the rent), and work units help workers to pay for their homes with cheap loans. But there are simply not enough homes for all the people who want them. Until the government can build more homes, people have to live in cramped conditions. The average amount of living space for each person in Shanghai is 4 metres by 6 metres – that's about the same size as two double beds.

The housing shortage has caused a lot of problems for young people and, in many cases, put pressure on their marriages. Because of this, the government of China has come up with an idea. Although Chunying and Lanying will probably have to wait between three and ten years for their own permanent place, in the meantime they can apply for a newly married couple's flat – but only for a year or two. If they have found nothing else in that period, they will have to return to Chunying's parents' house.

Governments today have to be able to adapt to many changes in society in order to provide for everyone. They may have very good ideas about solving the housing shortages but, at the end of the day, the problem can only be resolved by building more houses.

People in the countryside are also affected when a society becomes wealthier. Many people with good jobs in cities like to buy holiday homes in prettier or more peaceful parts of the country. The problem is that many of these pretty and peaceful places have fairly poor communities. The arrival of the wealthy newcomers causes property prices to go up. Often local people can no longer afford to buy homes in their own towns or villages.

Begging next to a shop sign may be the closest this woman will ever come to the 'high life'.

Homelessness in rural areas is a growing problem in many countries. A wealthy society does have many advantages. The standard of living for most people is high; they have modern conveniences, like vacuum cleaners and washing machines. They own cars which make getting around easier, and more people take holidays than ever before. Many people own their own homes. They have televisions, leisure time, education for all, and some kind of medical care. For many people life is good, full of choices and variety. People have to work extremely hard; the harder people work the more they seem to want. They no longer work just to pay for food and rent. They want bigger and better cars and houses, smarter clothes, more exotic holidays. There is a lot of pressure on people to succeed in the workplace, which leads to stress. Also, all these luxuries have a price: people borrow huge sums of money from banks and building societies, and run up huge bills on credit cards. Only one thing needs to go wrong, such as being made redundant or losing their jobs. What happens then? Who pays the huge debts, and the interest on the huge debts? People who find themselves in these situations very soon discover that they can no longer afford the 'good' life.

Today, in the modern world in which we live, people who, a short

In the early 1990s in the UK, many people could not pay their mortgages and, as a result, lost their homes.

time ago, had very good jobs are losing their homes. In Los Angeles, California, there are women from the upper classes who are living in their cars. When their marriages broke up, or they lost their jobs, they lost everything, including their homes. As much as anything else, homelessness is a result of the changes that are going on in society – what we call progress. If all the people in India or Africa wanted their own homes, like people in the West, before long there would be no space left in the world. In an already overcrowded world, we have to find solutions to the new problems which are facing us.

9

What can be done?

IN 1989, an organization in New York called Street Aid had an idea to help the homeless. They started *Street News*, a fortnightly newspaper which is produced and written by homeless people and is sold on the streets by homeless vendors. The vendor buys copies of the paper for 30 cents (about 22 pence) each. The vendor sells a copy of *Street News* for 75 cents (about 50 pence), giving him or her a profit of 45 cents (about 28 pence) per copy. There has been a lot of publicity about *Street News*, so many people know about it and are happy to buy the paper to help the homeless. After the paper had been running for a year, more than 100 of the vendors had found homes. Proceeds from sales of the paper had been put into a fund which helped the vendors with deposits for rent on apartments. This idea has since spread to other cities in the USA and to London, where the

Selling copies of The Big Issue *in Brighton, England. Proceeds from sales of the magazines are used to help the homeless.*

Former homeless people celebrate their graduation as chefs, in a restaurant in Atlantic City, USA. They were trained as part of the SMART scheme (Sites Made Available in Restaurant Training). Restaurant owners in the city set up the scheme to train homeless people as chefs and, hopefully, find jobs for them afterwards.

magazine *The Big Issue* is having similar success. New York has one of the worst homelessness problems in the developed world, but people in the city seem to come up with some of the brightest ideas. In the USA, people have to pay a deposit of a couple of cents for every bottle of fizzy drink or beer. The deposit is given back when the bottles are returned. In the fast-moving world of New York, many busy people do not have the time or cannot be bothered to save and return all their bottles. People who live on the streets and who have a lot of spare time are encouraged to collect any bottles they can find and return them to a central depot, where the deposit is paid directly to them. The aim of the scheme is not only to help homeless people to find some means of financial independence, but also to reduce the litter in New York's parks and public places, and to help the environment by returning more bottles for recycling.

Both the *Street News* and the bottle collecting schemes are effective as they recognize that two of the main problems experienced by homeless people are a lack of confidence and a lack of opportunities to improve their situations. By providing them with a chance to earn some money in a respectable way, the homeless can take the first step towards the chance of a better life. They gain confidence, and begin to feel that there is a way off the streets. Instead of being a drain on society, they are able to contribute in an important and effective way.

Charities which help the homeless with food and beds for the night are very important. Many also provide medical care, counselling and practical advice. But homeless people also need to be given a chance to participate in society. One of the more ingenious ideas for helping the homeless is an art workshop in London where homeless people can discover hidden talents. Again, this provides a much-needed confidence boost. Some companies have taken a small number of homeless people, given them a series of confidence-building workshops and training courses, helped them find accommodation and then taken them on as employees. Other organizations offer transitional housing. This is housing which is offered to homeless people for a short period of time. With a place to live, many find it easier to hold down jobs and build normal lives for themselves. In Brazil, some people involved in the churches have recognized that the best way to help the shanty town dwellers is to encourage them to organize into groups. As a group, they can help each other and work at ways to campaign for an improvement in their situation. They have had some significant successes, such as persuading the authorities to provide water services, and to build proper sewers through the shanty towns, which improves sanitation and reduces disease.

The media can play an important role in helping the homeless. Television programmes and newspaper articles pin-point individual cases, which draw the attention of the public and create pressure for governments to act.

In 1948, a few years after the end of the Second World War (1939-45), the governments of the world decided to do something about some of the world's most serious problems. They signed the *Universal Declaration of Human Rights*, a charter which was

For some people the pavement is a bed. People pass by: some look down but none help.

Homeless children in Durban, South Africa, sleeping under cardboard blankets.

designed to guarantee, for every citizen of the world, a minimum living standard, regardless of the family to which a person was born, or the country in which a person lived.

Article 25 of the Declaration stated that: 'Everyone has a right to a standard of living adequate for the health and well-being of himself and of his (or her) family, including food, clothing, housing and medical care and necessary social services, and the right to security in the event of unemployment, sickness, disability, widowhood, old age or other lack of livelihood in circumstances beyond his (or her) control.' Today, more than forty years after the Declaration was signed, the number of homeless people is still growing. It is estimated that there are now one billion homeless people worldwide. While the role of governments and international agencies such as the United Nations is important, they are not going to resolve the problem of homelessness completely. Governments have many other problems to deal with, and do not always have enough money to spend on building the number of houses that are needed.

There are wars, famines, tidal waves which cause homelessness and refugee crises everywhere. Small actions are as effective as grand widespread initiatives. We can all help. We can buy a copy of a newspaper for the homeless from street vendors. We can donate money to charities for the homeless. We can write letters to the press or to our members of parliament. Most importantly of all, we can remember that the homeless are people like us. We must do our best to make sure that they never give up hope. We must never forget that they are human beings with human rights.

Glossary

Bed and breakfast A type of accommodation where you receive a room in a private house and breakfast cooked by the owner. Recently the government has used this arrangement to house homeless people.
Breadwinner The person who supports the family with his or her earnings.
Corrupt Open to bribery.
Doss-house A cheap lodging-house, often used by tramps.
Evict To make a tenant leave a property.
Exploit To take advantage of someone or something.
Hostel A building where people can have a room for a night very cheaply. Hostels are often run by charitable organizations or governments.
Industrial Revolution The period during the eighteenth and nineteenth centuries in first Britain and then other Western European countries and the USA, when industries started to develop. The countries' main incomes came from industry rather than farming.
Lottery A game of chance run by the state where people can win huge prize money with the purchase of one ticket.
Pickpocket Someone who steals wallets and purses from people in public places.
Prostitute Someone who sells his or her body for sex.
Resident Someone who lives in a particular place or area.
Rickshaw A vehicle which is pulled by one or two people and is used in Asia as a taxi. Some are also motorized.
Rupee The currency of India.
Social security Financial assistance provided by the state for people who are unemployed or who don't earn much money.
Subsidized Available at a reduced price due to contributions by the government.
Welfare Financial and other assistance given to people in need.

Further reading

Human Rights by David Selby (Cambridge University Press, 1987)

Human Rights by Jane Sherwin (Wayland, 1989)

Let's Discuss Homelessness by Ann Kramer (Wayland, 1989)

Useful addresses

In Britain

British Institute of Human Rights
King's College, London
Faculty of Law
The Strand
London WC2R 2LS

Commonwealth Human Rights Initiative
27-28 Russell Square
London WC1B 5DS

Council for Education in World Citizenship
Seymour Mews House
Seymour Mews
London W1H 9PE

Minority Rights Group
29 Craven Street
London WC2N 5NT

Refugee Council
3 Bondway
London SW8 1SF

International

European Commission of Human Rights
Conseil de l'Europe
Boite Postale 431 R6
f-67006 Strasbourg Cedex
France

International Institute of Human Rights
1 Quai Lezay-Marnesia
f-67000 Strasbourg
France

International League for Human Rights
432 Park Avenue, S,
Room 1103
New York
NY 10016
USA

United Nations Human Rights Committee
U.N. Centre for Human Rights
Palais des Nations
CH-1211 Geneva 10
Switzerland

Index

Africa 8, 10, 41
Aid 35
Alcoholism on the streets 25, 26
Asia 10

Building more houses 40

Cities
   accommodation in 10-11, 18-19
   Bombay 15-17
   Budapest 38-9
   Cairo 34-5
   Delhi 19
   growth of 8, 10-11, 12
   industry in 10, 13
   London 22-4, 42
   Los Angeles 41
   Mexico City 12-14
   New York 42, 43
   overcrowding in 34, 39
   Paris 28-30
   Rio de Janeiro 20
   San Francisco 35-6
   Shanghai 39-40
Counselling for the homeless 44
Crime on the streets 19

Drugs on the streets 20, 25, 26

Earthquakes (as a cause of homelessness)
   in Cairo, Egypt 34-5
   in El Salvador 32-4
   in Naples, southern Italy 35
   in San Francisco, USA 35-6

Homelessness 4-6, 14
   charities which help 44, 45
   in Brazil 20-21
   in China 39-40
   in cities 5, 11, 15-21, 23-4, 32-6, 34-41, 42, 43
   in developed countries 22, 26, 28-30, 41, 42, 43
   in Egypt 34-5
   in El Salvador 32-4
   in Hungary 38-9
   in India 15-19
   in Los Angeles 41
   in Naples 35
   in Paris 28-30
   in San Francisco 35-6
   in the countryside 40-41
   reasons for 6, 7-9, 23, 24-5, 32-6, 37, 41, 45
   refugees 26
   schemes to combat 38-9, 42-5

Industrial Revolution in Europe 8

Latin America 10, 20-21, 44
Living on the streets 28-31
   alcoholics 25-6
   children 15-21
      in Brazil 20-21
      in India 15-19
   drug addicts 25-6
   mentally ill 27
   refugees 26

Population, growth of 10
Prostitution on the streets 19, 25
Public pressure for change 44

Refugees on the streets 26, 33

Scotland 22
Shanty towns 18, 34
Slums 18-19, 32, 34
Social services 22
Squats 22, 23
Street News 42, 43

The Big Issue 43, 44
'Tramps', treatment of 9

Universal Declaration of Human Rights 44-5

Workhouses 8-9